W9-CZS-644

How to Solve
Word Problems

Grades 6–8

Author

Robert Smith

Teacher Created Resources, Inc.
6421 Industry Way
Westminster, CA 92683
www.teachercreated.com

ISBN: 978-1-57690-961-4

©2000 Teacher Created Resources, Inc.
Reprinted, 2008
Made in U.S.A.

Table of Contents

A Note to Teachers and Parents

The design of this book is intended to allow it to be used by teachers or parents for a variety of purposes and needs. Each of the units contains one "How to" page and two or more practice pages. The "How to" section of each unit precedes the practice pages and provides needed information such as a concept or math rule to review, important terms and formulas to remember, or step-by-step guidelines necessary for using the practice pages.

About This Book

How to Solve Word Problems: *Grades 6–8* presents a comprehensive overview of strategies for solving word problems. The units include clear, simple, and readable instruction pages and student activities. This book, therefore, can be used as an instruction vehicle for introducing and teaching word problems to students with little or no background in the concepts. The units in this book can be used in whole-class instruction with the teacher or by a parent assisting his or her child through the book.

This book also lends itself to use by a small group doing remedial work on word problems or individuals and small groups in earlier grades engaged in enrichment or advanced work. A teacher may want to have two tracks within the class with one moving at a faster pace and the other at a gradual pace appropriate to the ability or background of his or her students. The units in this book can also be used in a learning center with materials specified for each unit of instruction.

Teachers and parents working with children who are new to the concept should take more time reviewing the "How to" pages with the children. Students should also be allowed to use a calculator to check the accuracy of their work. This reduces the need for correction and allows the material to be self-corrected, if desired.

If students have difficulty on a specific concept or unit within this book, review the material and allow them to redo the troublesome pages. Since concept development is sequential, it is not advisable to skip much of the material in the book. It is preferable that children find the work easy and gradually advance to the more difficult concepts.

It is very important that students develop a procedure for approaching word problems. The Five-Step Plan and Code Words introduced in Unit 1 provide students with effective tools for handling word problems. Other strategies are presented throughout the book.

Encourage students to use manipulatives to reinforce the concepts. They should use charts as well as other visual materials to find solutions to those word problems that they find difficult.

How to Solve Word Problems: *Grades 6–8* highlights the NCTM standard that the study of mathematics should emphasize problem solving in such a way that students can use problem-solving approaches to investigate and understand the general content of mathematics. Students are encouraged to solve problems involving everyday situations and real-life applications of math skills. These specific skills should help students develop strategies to solve a wide variety of math-related problems, to verify the accuracy and results of specific problems, and to acquire facility and confidence in making mathematics a meaningful enterprise for them.

This book is designed to match the suggestions of the National Council for the Teachers of Mathematics. They strongly support the learning of the four basic operations and other processes in the context of problem solving and real-world applications. Use every opportunity to have students apply these new skills in classroom situations and at home. This will reinforce the value of the skill as well as the process. This book matches a number of NCTM standards including these main topics and specific features:

Problem Solving

Students are asked to apply basic math computational skills in word problem formats with real-life applications. They develop aptitude and confidence in their computational ability and their ability to apply mathematics meaningfully. Students learn to apply basic math formulas effectively and correctly to problems rooted in real-life circumstances.

Communication

Students are given numerous opportunities to apply physical diagrams, charts, pictures, and materials to concrete mathematical ideas. Students can relate their everyday common language to the expression of mathematical ideas and symbols on a level appropriate to their age. Students will also understand that mathematics involves discussion, reading, writing, and listening as integral functions of mathematical instruction.

Reasoning

Students learn to apply logic to their math problems and to justify their answers. There is an emphasis on recognizing patterns as a way of approaching problem solving as well as the use of models, manipulatives, and charts. Students learn specific, effective, concrete strategies for solving unconventional problems and problems with several facets which require organization and unusual approaches to problem solving.

Connections

Students are encouraged to recognize and relate various mathematical concepts, processes, and patterns to each other. They are likewise encouraged to use mathematics across the curriculum and in their daily lives.

Other Standards

This book is well aligned with other NCTM standards which stress instruction of whole-number computation and learning geometrical concepts through word problem applications and that fractions, decimals, and measurement be taught or reinforced with real-life and word-problem applications.

1 ► How to ••••• Apply Problem-Solving Techniques with Single-Step Problems

Facts to Know

Solving word problems isn't a matter of luck or guesswork. You just have to do the work step by step following a simple plan like this one.

Use this simple Five-Step Plan to help you solve the word problems in this book.

Five-Step Plan

> 1. Read the problem carefully.
> 2. State the problem to be solved.
> 3. Determine the operation to be used.
> 4. Do the operation.
> 5. Check the answer to see if it is reasonable.
>
> ★ ★ ★ ★ Don't skip any steps! ★ ★ ★ ★

1. **Read the problem carefully**. Check the meaning of words you don't know. You may need to read the problem again perhaps more slowly. Read the problem in parts—either every few words or every sentence. Use periods and commas as a guide.

2. **State the problem to be solved**. Restate the problem in your own words. Use the fewest possible words to describe what you have to find out. Talk it out with yourself or write it out in one or two sentences.

3. **Determine the operation to be used**. There are only four operations: addition, subtraction, multiplication, and division. Use the Code Word list to help you. Choose the most likely operation using all the clues you have found.

4. **Do the operation**. Check to see that no careless errors have been made and that your math facts are accurate.

5. **Check the answer to see if it is reasonable**. Compare your answer to the original problem to see if it makes sense.

Code Words

Study the words listed below each operation and use this list when you are doing the problems in this book. These words usually—but not always—indicate the operation to be used.

Addition +	Subtraction –	Multiplication x	Division ÷
altogether	change	times	split evenly
in all	how much more	compute the area	divided by
sum	difference	product	quotient
perimeter	how much less	find the volume	find the average
entire cost	how many fewer	percent	batting average
total	minus	times as many as	passing percentage
total cost	how much left	% of discount	shared evenly
	how much saved	% of tax	
	how much taller		
	how much older		

Five-Step Plan

1. Read the problem carefully.
2. State the problem to be solved.
3. Determine the operation to be used.
4. Do the operation.
5. Check the answer to see if it is reasonable.

Directions: Use the Five-Step Plan and the Code Words from page 5 to help you solve the following word problems.

1. You gave a clerk a $10.00 bill to pay for a pair of socks that cost $7.88. How much change should you receive?

   I have to find out:_____

   _____

   Operation to use: _____

   Answer: _____

2. Robin's mother bought 16 burger and fry combos at the Burger Barn for a party. Each combo cost $2.29. How much did she spend?

   I have to find out:_____

   _____

   Operation to use: _____

   Answer: _____

3. Mike and 7 friends were given a huge box containing 224 old baseball cards. Mike divided the cards evenly among all 8 friends. How many cards did each person receive?

   I have to find out:_____

   _____

   Operation to use: _____

   Answer: _____

4. Kevin has saved $49.67 toward a new skateboard. The board he wants costs $60.00. How much more money does he need?

   I have to find out:_____

   _____

   Operation to use: _____

   Answer: _____

5. Mary bought some tennis shoes for $59.67, a pair of jeans for $29.95, and a watch for $39.55. How much money did Mary spend in all?

   I have to find out:_____

   _____

   Operation to use: _____

   Answer: _____

6. Rachel bought a CD on sale by her favorite group for $15.78. It usually sells for $17.99. How much did she save at the sale price?

   I have to find out:_____

   _____

   Operation to use: _____

   Answer: _____

7. Gas sells for $1.89 a gallon. How much will it cost to buy 22 gallons at this price?

   I have to find out:_____

   _____

   Operation to use: _____

   Answer: _____

Directions: Use Code Words and the Five-Step Plan on page 5 to help you solve these problems.

1. You went into the Free-Wheeler Bicycle Shop to buy some riding shorts. They cost $33.89. How much change did you get from a $50.00 dollar bill?

   I have to find out:_____

   _____

   Operation to use: _____

   Answer: _____

2. A new mountain bicycle costs $299.00, but you can get a 20% discount if you belong to a biking club. How much money would the discount be?

   I have to find out:_____

   _____

   Operation to use: _____

   Answer: _____

3. You purchased some new knee pads for $7.78, a water bottle for $4.50, a new seat for $25.89, and riding gloves for $12.56. What was the total cost of your purchases?

   I have to find out:_____

   _____

   Operation to use: _____

   Answer: _____

4. The fee for entering the last bike race was $25.00 for each rider. The organizers collected 213 times as much money. How much money was collected?

   I have to find out:_____

   _____

   Operation to use: _____

   Answer: _____

5. You rode 88.24 miles in an 8-hour period. What was the average number of miles you rode in one hour?

   I have to find out:_____

   _____

   Operation to use: _____

   Answer: _____

6. Your family bought a mountain bike for $429.00, a 15-speed bike for $567.98, and a tandem bike for $345.99. What was the total cost?

   I have to find out:_____

   _____

   Operation to use: _____

   Answer: _____

7. You spent $19.45 for repairs in the Free-Wheeler Bike Shop one morning. Another customer spent 18 times as much money as you did. How much money did the other customer spend?

   I have to find out:_____

   _____

   Operation to use: _____

   Answer: _____

8. You rode 30.5 miles one day, 22.3 miles the second day, 43.4 miles the third day, and 29.1 miles the fourth day. What was the total number of miles that you rode during the 4 days?

   I have to find out:_____

   _____

   Operation to use: _____

   Answer: _____

CD Blastaway is the newest store selling all the hit CD albums and singles. It caters to every kind of musical taste and even carries albums your parents would listen to.

Directions: Use Code Words and the Five-Step Plan to help you solve these word problems.

1. The latest fan favorite is a group called Outta Time. You can buy their latest album for $11.95 at CD Blastaway. How much change would you receive from a 20-dollar bill?

   I have to find out:_____

   _____

   Operation to use: _____

   Answer: _____

2. A double album by the new pop sensation, Asparagus, costs $27.95 at most stores, but Blastaway has it on sale for $21.00. How much would you save at CD Blastaway?

   I have to find out:_____

   _____

   Operation to use: _____

   Answer: _____

3. You have decided to cover one wall of your room with 23 posters of your favorite group, Moody and the Goldfish. Each poster costs $4.95. What is the product of 23 and $4.95?

   I have to find out:_____

   _____

   Operation to use: _____

   Answer: _____

4. Your mother gave you a $50.00 bill to buy a triple album of your dad's favorite group, the Lightning Bugs. It cost $24.59. How much money did you have left?

   I have to find out _____

   _____

   Operation to use: _____

   Answer: _____

5. You and 9 of your friends decide to buy a $15.90 CD for your math teacher and split the cost evenly. How much did each of you spend?

   I have to find out:_____

   _____

   Operation to use: _____

   Answer: _____

6. CD Blastaway draws your name as the winner of a trunk of old CDs. You decide to share the 324 CDs in the trunk evenly among 12 people, including yourself. How many CDs does each person receive?

   I have to find out:_____

   _____

   Operation to use: _____

   Answer: _____

7. You are offered a 20% discount on the latest album by the Me Too You rap group which usually sells for $15.95. How much money is the discount?

   I have to find out:_____

   _____

   Operation to use: _____

   Answer: _____

8. What is the difference in price between a CD costing $11.99 and a CD costing $8.88?

   I have to find out _____

   _____

   Operation to use: _____

   Answer: _____

Facts to Know

Some word problems follow a pattern that usually indicates what operation to use.

Addition Pattern

Word problems with a list usually indicate addition. Examples include the following:

- list of prices
- list of amounts of money
- list of items purchased
- list of lengths
- list of widths
- list of one kind of measurement
- different amounts of one object
- list of scores

Sample

Jennifer bought a yellow blouse for $16.98, a pair of blue jeans for $29.99, a skirt for $38.50, and a pair of shoes for $55.78. How much money did she spend?

$16.98 + $29.99 + $38.50 + $55.78 = $141.25

She spent $141.25.

Subtraction Pattern

Word problems that compare usually indicate subtraction. Examples include the following:

- how much more
- how much less
- how much longer
- how much shorter
- how much bigger
- how much smaller

Sample

Sam is 59 inches tall. Jonathan is 73 inches tall. How much taller is Jonathan?

73 − 59 = 14

Jonathan is 14 inches taller.

Multiplication Pattern

Word problems that name the cost or measurement of one item and ask for the cost or measurement of several of the same items usually indicate multiplication.

Sample

One medium cola at Burger Barn costs $0.79. How much do 20 medium colas cost?

$0.79 x 20 = $15.80

The cost of 20 medium colas is $15.80.

Division Pattern

If something is being split among several people or being averaged, division is usually indicated.

Sample

Dinner for 8 adults at the Pasta Palace costs $88.80. If the 8 adults split the cost evenly, how much would each adult pay?

$$
\begin{array}{r}
\$11.10 \\
8\overline{)\$88.80} \\
\underline{-8} \\
08 \\
\underline{-8} \\
08 \\
\underline{-8} \\
0
\end{array}
$$

Each adult paid $11.10.

Pandora's Pizza Emporium Menu

Cheese Pizza	$7.50	Pepperoni Pizza	$9.98
Pineapple Pizza	$9.50	Veggie Pizza	$8.95
Sausage Pizza	$7.99	Anchovy Pizza	$11.50
Hot Pepper Pizza	$7.99	Kitchen-Sink Pizza	$15.00

Directions: Use the information on page 9 and the menu shown above to solve these problems.

1. Your soccer coach bought a cheese pizza, a pepperoni pizza, a sausage pizza, and a veggie pizza to celebrate your latest victory. How much did the coach spend?

   Pattern: _____

   Answer: _____

2. Your mother bought a veggie pizza and an anchovy pizza. How much more did she spend on the anchovy pizza?

   Pattern: _____

   Answer: _____

3. The principal at your school bought a cheese pizza and a kitchen-sink pizza which has everything on it. How much more expensive was the kitchen-sink pizza?

   Pattern: _____

   Answer: _____

4. The science teacher bought a kitchen-sink pizza, a sausage pizza, a pepperoni pizza, and a cheese pizza to test student pizza preferences. How much did the teacher spend on pizza?

   Pattern: _____

   Answer: _____

5. How much less does an anchovy pizza cost than a kitchen-sink pizza?

   Pattern: _____

   Answer: _____

6. Your language arts teacher bought one of every kind of pizza. What was her total cost?

   Pattern: _____

   Answer: _____

7. Make a list of four pizzas you would buy. How much would it cost you altogether?

   Pattern: _____

   Answer: _____

10

Pandora's Pizza Emporium Menu			
Cheese Pizza	$7.50	Pepperoni Pizza	$9.98
Pineapple Pizza	$9.50	Veggie Pizza	$8.95
Sausage Pizza	$7.99	Anchovy Pizza	$11.50
Hot Pepper Pizza	$7.99	Kitchen-Sink Pizza	$15.00

Directions: Use the information on page 9 and the menu above to solve these problems.

1. The basketball coach bought 6 cheese pizzas. How much did he spend?

   Pattern: _____

   Answer: _____

2. Four friends bought a kitchen-sink pizza and split the cost evenly. How much did each friend pay?

   Pattern: _____

   Answer: _____

3. The seventh-grade history teacher bought 11 anchovy pizzas for the history club. How much did it cost her?

   Pattern: _____

   Answer: _____

4. A group of 10 sixth-grade students each bought a pepperoni pizza. How much did it cost for the 10 pizzas?

   Pattern: _____

   Answer: _____

5. A cheese pizza and soft drink combo costs $7.95. How much did the soccer coach pay for 15 combos?

   Pattern: _____

   Answer: _____

6. A group of 5 teachers bought a veggie pizza and shared the cost evenly. How much did each teacher spend?

   Pattern: _____

   Answer: _____

Challenge

- A group of 4 teachers bought 6 cheese pizzas. They shared the cost evenly. How much did each teacher spend? _____

- A group of 12 parents bought 7 kitchen-sink pizzas. They divided the cost evenly. How much did it cost each parent? _____

```
┌──────────────────────────────────────────────────────────────┐
│                      Tornado Tacos Menu                        │
│                                                                │
│   Tornado Taco          $1.89      Large Cola        $2.39     │
│   Double Bean Burrito   $2.49      Double Cola       $3.99     │
│   Red-eyed Chili        $4.59                                  │
└──────────────────────────────────────────────────────────────┘
```

Directions: Use the information on page 9 and the menu above to help you solve these problems.

1. Your best friend bought 12 Tornado Tacos for a party. How much did they cost your friend?

   Pattern: _____

   Answer: _____

2. Jennifer bought a Tornado Taco, a Double Bean Burrito, and Red-eyed Chili. What was her total cost?

   Pattern: _____

   Answer: _____

3. Your next door neighbor bought 13 Red-eyed Chilies for a party. How much did he spend?

   Pattern: _____

   Answer: _____

4. Your mom bought Red-eyed Chili, a Double Bean Burrito, a large cola, and a double cola. What was her bill?

   Pattern: _____

   Answer: _____

5. The total bill for a group of eight coaches at Tornado Tacos was $136.32. They decided to split the cost evenly among the eight of them. How much did each coach pay?

   Pattern: _____

   Answer: _____

6. How much less does a Tornado Taco cost than a Red-eyed Chili?

   Pattern: _____

   Answer: _____

Challenge

• What is the total cost of eight Tornado Tacos and 12 Red-eyed Chilies? _____

• What foods could you buy for exactly $6.77?

  _____

• How much less does one Red-eyed Chili cost than 2 Double Bean Burritos? _____

Facts to Know

Addition and Subtraction with Fractions and Mixed Numbers

- Fractions and mixed numbers need to be arranged in the ladder form (one above the other) before adding or subtracting.
- Find the common denominator for fractions with unlike denominators.
- The common denominator is the least common multiple of the two denominators.
- Reduce (simplify) all answers to the lowest terms.

Sample A (Fractions)   **Sample B** (Mixed Numbers)

$$\frac{3}{4} + \frac{5}{6} =$$

$$\frac{9}{12} + \frac{10}{12} = \frac{19}{12} \text{ or } 1\frac{7}{12}$$

$$12\frac{7}{8} - 5\frac{1}{4} =$$

$$12\frac{7}{8} - 5\frac{2}{8} = 7\frac{5}{8}$$

Multiplication of Fractions and Mixed Numbers

- Fractions are multiplied side by side.
- "Of" usually means multiply in word problems. ($\frac{1}{3}$ of . . .)
- Cancel any numerator that will divide evenly into any denominator or any denominator that will cancel into a numerator.
- Canceling fractions is a way to reduce (simplify) the problem to lower terms.
- Canceling often (but not always) makes it unnecessary to reduce (simplify) the answer.
- Mixed numbers and whole numbers must be converted to improper fractions before they can be multiplied.
- Mixed numbers can be converted to improper fractions by multiplying the denominator times the whole number and adding the numerator. ($3\frac{1}{2} = \frac{7}{2}$)
- Whole numbers are converted to fractions by using 1 as the denominator. ($3 = \frac{3}{1}$)

Sample C (Fractions)

$$\overset{1}{\cancel{\frac{2}{8}}} \times \overset{1}{\underset{5}{\cancel{\frac{4}{15}}}} =$$
$$\underset{2}{}$$

$$\frac{1}{2} \times \frac{1}{5} = \frac{1}{10}$$

Sample D (Mixed Numbers)

$$2\frac{1}{4} \times 2\frac{2}{5} =$$

$$\underset{1}{\cancel{\frac{9}{4}}} \times \overset{3}{\cancel{\frac{12}{5}}} =$$

$$\frac{9}{1} \times \frac{3}{5} = \frac{27}{5} = 5\frac{2}{5}$$

Division of Fractions and Mixed Numbers

- Fractions are divided side by side.
- Fractions are divided by finding the reciprocal of the second term and multiplying.
- The reciprocal of a fraction reverses the position of the numerator and the denominator. $\frac{2}{3}$ and $\frac{3}{2}$ are reciprocals.
- Reciprocals are two fractions that multiply to a product of 1.

Sample E (Fractions)

$$\frac{3}{5} \div \frac{1}{2} =$$

$$\frac{3}{5} \times \frac{2}{1} = \frac{6}{5} = 1\frac{1}{5}$$

Shaping Up

You and your friends are getting ready to try out for the team sports at your school. You're pushing away the second helpings of dessert and doing push-ups instead. You're running the track instead of using the remote control for the television set.

Directions: Use the information on page 13 to help you solve these problems.

1. You start running every other day to get in shape gradually. On Monday you ran $\frac{1}{3}$ of a mile and on Wednesday you ran $\frac{3}{4}$ of a mile. How far did you run in all? _____

2. You ran $1\frac{2}{3}$ miles on Friday and your best friend ran $1\frac{1}{4}$ miles. How much farther did you run?

   _____

3. The track you are using is $\frac{2}{3}$ of a mile long. How far would you run if you took 4 laps around the track? _____

4. The track is $\frac{2}{3}$ of a mile in length. How far do you run if you run $\frac{1}{2}$ of the track? _____

5. The quarterback on the football team ran $2\frac{1}{3}$ miles. The wide receiver ran $\frac{1}{2}$ of that distance. How far did the wide receiver run? _____

6. When you try out for the cross-country team, you have to run 12 laps to make the team. Each lap is $\frac{2}{3}$ of a mile. How far do you run? _____

7. A forward on the basketball team ran $6\frac{1}{4}$ miles over a 5-day period. He ran exactly the same distance each day. How far did he run each day? _____

8. You ran $1\frac{5}{6}$ miles on Saturday and $2\frac{4}{9}$ miles on Sunday. How far did you run altogether?

   _____

9. Your friend ran $3\frac{1}{6}$ miles on a day when you ran $2\frac{2}{3}$ miles. How much farther did your friend run? _____

10. A halfback ran $2\frac{2}{3}$ miles every day for 10 days. How many miles did he run altogether? _____

Extension

- Keep a record of the number of miles you run on a track or a measured route for a week.

- Compute the total number of miles you ran.

- Calculate the average number of miles or partial miles you ran each day.

Party Time

Your mother decides to have a pizza party to celebrate your birthday. All of the pizzas are the same size although the toppings are different. You get to invite all of your friends.

Directions: Use the information on page 13 to help you solve these problems.

1. You ate $\frac{1}{6}$ of a cheese pizza, $\frac{1}{3}$ of a pepperoni pizza, and $\frac{1}{4}$ of a sausage pizza. How much pizza did you eat altogether? _____

2. Your mother had a punch bottle with 65 ounces of fruit punch. How many $6\frac{1}{2}$ ounce cups could she fill from this bottle? _____

3. When she started to serve the pizza, your mother gave $\frac{1}{4}$ of a pizza to each of the 15 people at the party. How much pizza did she serve?_____

4. Your best friend ate $\frac{3}{8}$ of a pizza from 4 different pizzas. How much pizza did he eat?_____

5. A group of 3 of your friends divided $1\frac{1}{2}$ pizzas among them. How much did each friend eat? _____

6. Your mother made several small birthday cakes. You ate $\frac{3}{10}$ of a cake and your best friend ate $\frac{2}{5}$ of a cake. How much more did your friend eat? _____

7. One of the boys ate $\frac{9}{16}$ of a cake and another ate $\frac{3}{8}$ of a cake. How much did they eat altogether? _____

8. Your mother had a 49-ounce bag of your favorite candy pieces called Bitabits. How many $3\frac{1}{2}$ ounce cups could she fill with Bitabits?_____

9. There were 20 people at your party. They ate $12\frac{1}{2}$ pizzas. What was the average amount of pizza eaten by each partygoer?_____

10. Each piece of cake was $2\frac{1}{4}$ ounces and 36 pieces were eaten. How many ounces of cake were eaten? _____

11. Each cup of punch had $6\frac{1}{2}$ ounces. There were 52 cups of punch. How many ounces of punch were served? _____

12. A group of 3 girls shared $4\frac{1}{2}$ ounces of cake. How many ounces of cake did each girl eat?_____

Extension

The partygoers ate $12\frac{1}{2}$ pizzas. Of this amount, $4\frac{1}{3}$ were pepperoni pizzas and $3\frac{1}{2}$ were cheese pizzas. The remaining pizzas were sausage pizzas. How many sausage pizzas were eaten? _____

3 ▶ Practice ••••• Solving Even More Word Problems with Fractions and Mixed Numbers

Ride On!

You and your family go on a camping and riding vacation to a national park. You get to do a lot of bike riding through some rough trails and along some scenic bike routes.

Directions: Use the information on page 13 to help you solve these problems.

1. You and 4 of your friends rode your bikes on a $6\frac{3}{4}$ mile trip to a lake before lunch. What was the total miles that all 5 of you rode? _____

2. You rode up a long mountainous trail that was $3\frac{7}{8}$ miles long. Your mother took a gentler trail that was $2\frac{9}{10}$ miles in length. How much farther did you ride? _____

3. You and a friend start on different trails and agree to meet at noon for lunch at a favorite camping ground. You traveled $4\frac{3}{5}$ miles along your route. Your friend's route was only $3\frac{9}{10}$ miles in length. How much farther did you travel? _____

4. Your mother divided $4\frac{1}{2}$ pounds of high-energy trail mix among 9 bicyclists before a day trip. How much trail mix did each bicyclist receive? _____

5. You rode a total of $6\frac{1}{3}$ miles on Monday, $4\frac{1}{2}$ miles on Tuesday, and $3\frac{5}{6}$ miles on Wednesday. How many miles did you ride in all? _____

6. You ate $\frac{3}{4}$ of a pound of dried nuts and fruits each day for 12 days. How much of this food did you eat in the 12 days? _____

7. You rode $23\frac{1}{3}$ miles of dirt trail in 5 days. What was your average daily mileage? _____

8. You raced down a steep downhill track in $11\frac{4}{5}$ seconds. Your friend took $13\frac{1}{8}$ seconds. How many seconds faster were you? _____

9. The bike route around a lake was $2\frac{3}{4}$ miles. You rode $4\frac{1}{2}$ times around the lake. How far did you ride? _____

10. Your longest ride was $15\frac{1}{8}$ miles. Your shortest ride was $7\frac{5}{12}$ miles. What was the difference? _____

Extension

Keep a daily record of how far you ride a bike, a scooter, or a skateboard for a week. You can estimate a regular block as $\frac{1}{10}$ of a mile.

• Compute your total mileage for the week.

• Calculate your average daily mileage for the week.

• Multiply your weekly mileage by $4\frac{1}{3}$ to determine your monthly mileage.

How to • • • • • • • • • • • • • • • • • Solve Word Problems with Decimals and Percentages

Facts to Know

When doing word problems involving decimals:

- Use the Five-Step Plan.
- Look for Word-Problem Patterns.

- Check for Code Words.
- Do the Decimal Operations.

Decimal Operations

Addition and Subtraction

In addition and subtraction problems involving decimals, align the numbers with the decimal points directly above or below each other. Use the ladder form (one number on top of another).

correct	incorrect
5.67	5.67
+ 12.9	+ 12.9

Multiplication

In multiplying with decimals, use the ladder form.

When multiplying decimals, count all of the places to the right of the decimal points in the problem and place the decimal point in the answer so that the same number of places are to the right of the decimal point.

$$\begin{array}{r} 3.41 \\ \times\ .9 \\ \hline 3.069 \end{array}$$

two places to the left, plus one place to the left in the problem which equals three places to the left in the answer

Money is never multiplied by money.

correct	incorrect
$3.45	$3.45
x 1.95	x $1.95

Division

When you divide a whole number into a decimal, place the decimal point directly above the decimal point in the dividend.

$$6\overline{)12.6} = 2.1$$

When a problem has a decimal point in the divisor, move the decimal point to the right until the divisor is a whole number. Move the decimal point in the dividend the same number of places to the right.

$$.5\overline{)2.5} \qquad 5.\overline{)25.} = 5.$$

Use one or more zeroes to add places in the dividend, if needed, to move the decimal point.

$$.11\overline{)2.2} \qquad 11.\overline{)220} = 20.$$

Percents and Percentages

When you want to compute a percent of a number, change the percent to the equivalent decimal and multiply.

$$\begin{array}{r} 50 \\ \times\ .20 \\ \hline 10.00 \end{array}$$ 20% of 50 is 10

Percentages are computed by dividing a part by the whole.

6/20 is converted to a percentage by dividing 6 by 20.

$$20\overline{)6.00} = .30 \qquad .30 = 30\% \text{ of } 60$$

Add two zeroes after the decimal point, if necessary, to express the answer in hundredths.

Round the answer to the nearest hundredth.

Drop the decimal point and add the percentage sign.

Shopping Spree

Sandy's parents gave her $300.00 to buy new school clothes before she began middle school. She had to buy enough to last for the year, and she couldn't spend more than $30.00 for any single piece of clothing.

Directions: Use the information from page 17 to help you compute Sandy's costs. Starting with $300.00, determine how much money is remaining after each purchase. (*Hint*: Subtract the cost of the clothing bought from the money leftover from the previous answer.)

Sandy's School Clothes Purchases	Amount Remaining $300.00
1. Sandy bought a pair of blue jeans for $19.95, a pair of shorts for $12.35, and a skirt for $29.99. What was the total cost? How much money is left?	– _____ =
2. Sandy purchased five different colored tops at a price of $15.50 each. What was the total cost? How much money is left?	– _____ =
3. She bought 12 pairs of socks for $0.99 per pair. How much did the socks cost? How much money is left?	– _____ =
4. Sandy purchased a dress that ordinarily cost $37.28, but it was on sale for a 20% discount. How much was the discount? How much did the dress actually cost? How much money is left?	– _____ =
5. She purchased a pair of tennis shoes for $29.99 and a pair of sandals for $27.95. How much did she spend on footwear? How much money is left?	– _____ =
6. She bought two nylon jackets that ordinarily cost $40.00 a piece. They were each on sale at 25% off. How much was the discount for each jacket? How much did the jackets actually cost? How much money is left?	– _____ =

7. How much did Sandy spend on all of her school clothes together? _____

8. Did Sandy ever spend more than $30.00 for any item of clothing? _____

Basketball Tryouts

A local community club is offering tryouts for all interested students at its middle school basketball camp. Everyone is welcome.

Directions: Use the information on page 17 to help you solve these word problems. The first two have been started for you.

1. You took 20 shots in your first workout and made 12 of them. What was your shooting percentage? _____

   $$20\overline{)12.00}$$

2. Your best friend made 60% of the 40 shots she took. How many shots did your friend make? _____

   $$\begin{array}{r} 40 \\ \times\ .60 \\ \hline \end{array}$$

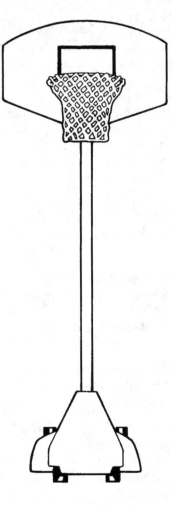

3. Hi Lowe shot 35 times and made 25 shots. What was his shooting percentage? _____

4. Julie Shootsalott made 34% of her 50 shots. How many shots did she make? _____

5. Swish Malone took 28 shots and made 25 of them. What was his shooting percentage? _____

6. Slammin' Sammy made 95% of his 20 shots. How many shots did he make? _____

7. Lightning Lizzy made 34 out of 36 shots taken. What was her shooting percentage? _____

8. Your team made 44 of 68 shots in its first game. What was the team shooting percentage? _____

9. Your opponents made 39 out of 61 shots. What was their shooting percentage? _____

10. In your last game, you made 16% of 25 shots taken. How many shots did you make? _____

Extension

Compute your own shooting percentage from a game or some playground shoot-around. Indicate the number of shots taken, the number of shots made, and your shooting percentage.

Your Body

Directions: Use the information on page 17 to help you solve these problems.

1. A human male has 1.5 gallons of blood in his body. A female has 0.875 gallons of blood in her body. How much more blood does the male have? _____

2. About 18% of the weight of the human body is bone. How many pounds of bone would a 140-pound person have? _____

3. The average brain weight of a male is 49.4 ounces. The average brain weight of a female is 45 ounces. How much heavier is the male brain? (Brain weight has nothing to do with intelligence.) _____

4. About 36% of female body weight is muscle. How many pounds of muscle would a 120-pound girl have? _____

5. On average, a 25-year-old male can hold 6.8 quarts of air in his lungs, and a 25-year-old female can hold 4.4 quarts of air. How much more air do the lungs in the average male hold? _____

6. Water accounts for about 62% of an individual's total body weight. How many pounds of water would a 185-pound person have? _____

7. Fat accounts for about 15% of total body weight. How many pounds of fat would a 130-pound person have? _____

8. Blood takes about 16 seconds to be pumped from the heart to the toes and back again. How many times would the blood be pumped in 1 minute (60 seconds)? _____

9. The pulse of an average person indicates 72 heart beats per minute. A skilled swimmer has a pulse rate of 40 beats per minute. The swimmer's pulse rate is what percentage of the average person's pulse rate? _____

10. One human eyelash lives about 150 days. What percentage of a year does the eyelash live? _____

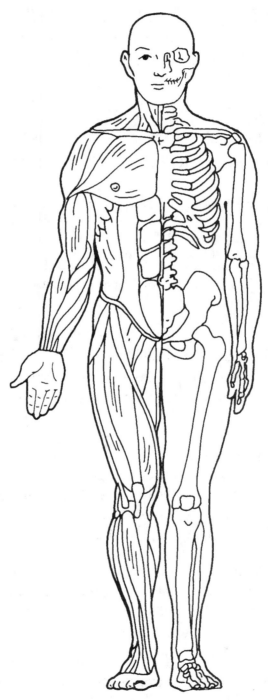

Facts to Know

Basic Geometric Formulas

Perimeter

- Perimeter is the length around a closed shape. It is computed by adding the length of all the sides of the figure.

- The formula for finding the perimeter of rectangles and other parallelograms is $P = (l + w) \times 2$ or $P = 2\,l + 2\,w$

Area

The area of a flat surface is a measure of how much space is covered by that surface. Area is measured in square units.

- **Area of a Rectangle**

  The area of a rectangle is computed by multiplying the width of one side times the length of the adjoining side.
  $A = l \times w$

  The area of a rectangle can also be determined by multiplying the base times the height.
  $A = b \times h$

- **Area of a Triangle**

  A triangle is always one half of a rectangle or a parallelogram. The area of a triangle is computed by multiplying 1/2 of the base times the height of a triangle.
  $A = \frac{1}{2} b \times h$

- **Area of a Parallelogram**

  The area of a parallelogram is computed by multiplying the base times the height.
  $A = b \times h$

- **Area of a Circle**

  To find the area of a circle, multiply π (3.14) times the radius times the radius again.
  $A = \pi\, r^2$

Circumference

The circumference is the distance around a circle. To find the circumference of a circle, multiply π (which always equals 3.14) times the diameter or multiply 2 times π (3.14) times the radius.

$$C = \pi\, d \ \text{ or } \ C = 2\,\pi\, r$$

Volume

- The formula for finding the volume of a rectangular prism, such as a box, is to multiply the length times the width times the height. $V = l \times w \times h$

- The formula for finding the volume of a cylinder is to multiply π (3.14) times the radius squared times the height. $V = \pi \times r^2 \times h$

- Volume is always computed in cubic units. Use cubic inches or centimeters when determining volume for small prisms and cylinders, and cubic feet or meters for larger ones.

Geometry at Home

Geometry is a very important aspect of math around the home. Houses and property are measured in geometric terms. Floor and wall coverings, heating systems, and the water supply all have a geometric component.

For this practice page, you need to know the following:

- Wallpaper is sold in double rolls totaling 44 square feet.
- Carpeting is priced by the square yard.
- There are 9 square feet in 1 square yard.
- You cannot buy partial rolls of carpeting or wallpaper.

Directions: Use the formulas and information on page 21 and the information above to help you solve these word problems.

1. Your mother said you can have new carpeting in your room if you compute the amount of carpeting needed and the cost. The length of your room is $18\frac{1}{2}$ feet and the width is 17 feet.

   The cost of one medium grade of carpeting is $20.00 per square yard.

   A. Compute the number of square feet in the room: _____

   B. Convert square feet to square yards (divide by 9): _____

   C. Compute the cost of carpeting needed (multiply by $20.00): _____

2. You want to cover one wall of your room with neon-colored wallpaper that costs $25.00 for a double roll containing 44 square feet. The wall is $18\frac{1}{2}$ feet long and 10 feet high.

   A. Compute the area of your wall in square feet. _____

   B. Determine how many rolls of wallpaper you need: _____

   C. Compute the cost of the wallpaper: _____

3. Your friend decided to paint the walls and the ceiling of her room with a lovely lavender paint. One gallon of this paint will cover only 400 square feet and costs $17.99 a gallon. These are the dimensions of her room:

   - Wall 1—$21\frac{1}{4}$ feet long and $11\frac{1}{2}$ feet high
   - Wall 3—$21\frac{1}{4}$ feet long and $11\frac{1}{2}$ feet high
   - Wall 2—20 feet long and $11\frac{1}{2}$ feet high
   - Wall 4—20 feet long and $11\frac{1}{2}$ feet high
   - Ceiling—$21\frac{1}{4}$ feet long and 20 feet wide

   A. Compute the area of each wall and ceiling in square feet.

   Wall 1 _____ Wall 2 _____ Wall 3 _____ Wall 4 _____ Ceiling _____

   B. Compute the total area in square feet: _____

   C. Determine how many gallons of paint are needed: _____

   D. Compute the total cost of the paint: _____

Solving More Word Problems with Geometry

Neighborhood Jobs

You need money to supplement your allowance. You decide to pick up some jobs at home and in the neighborhood so you can buy some necessities such as a scooter, a mountain bike, and a boom box.

Directions: Use the formulas and information on page 21 to help you solve these word problems.

1. Your dad agrees to pay you for mowing the front and back lawn. He will pay you $0.01 a square foot. The front lawn is 62 feet long and 38 feet wide.

   A. What is the square footage? _____
   B. How much will you be paid? _____

2. Your dad will pay you $0.03 a linear foot for trimming the edge of this lawn.

   A. What is the perimeter of the lawn? ____
   B. How much will you be paid? _____

3. The back lawn is shaped like a parallelogram. The base is 36 feet and the height is 31 feet.

   A. What is the square footage? _____
   B. How much will you be paid? _____

4. Your next-door neighbor offers to pay you the same price for edging and mowing his circular lawn which has a radius of 5.5 feet.

   A. What is the circumference of the lawn? _____
   B. How much will you be paid for edging? _____
   C. What is the area of the lawn in square feet? _____
   D. How much will you be paid for mowing it? _____

5. A neighbor down the street offers to pay you $0.15 a square foot to paint his fence which is 103 feet long and 6.25 feet high. He will supply the paint.

   A. What is the square footage? _____
   B. How much will you be paid? _____

6. Your favorite uncle offers to pay you $0.18 a square foot to paint his board fence. It is $8\frac{1}{2}$ feet high and 26 feet long.

   A. What is the square footage? _____
   B. How much will you be paid? _____

7. A neighboring mother wants you to paint a dodge ball court with a 6-foot radius on her driveway.

   A. What is the circumference of the court? _____
   B. What is the area in square feet of the court? _____

Extension

• Measure and compute the perimeter and area of your lawn.
• Measure and compute the perimeter and area of a neighbor's lawn.

Directions: Use the formulas and information on page 21 to help you solve these word problems.

1. You decide to start your own sidewalk business after school selling candy bars. The candy bars come packed in cartons which are 1 foot long, 1 foot wide, and 1 foot high (a cubic foot). How many of these cartons could you pack into your closet which is 5 feet long, 4 feet wide, and 12 feet high? _____

2. Your bedroom is 20 feet wide, $18\frac{1}{2}$ feet long, and 11 feet high. How many cubic feet of space are in your bedroom? _____

3. The circular top of your water heater has a radius of 9 inches. The height of the cylinder is 8 feet 5 inches. How many cubic inches of water will the water heater hold? _____

4. A can of cleanser has a radius of 4.5 cm and a height of 22.3 cm. How many cubic centimeters of cleanser will the can hold? _____

5. A closet in your parent's bedroom is $9\frac{1}{4}$ feet long, $3\frac{1}{3}$ feet wide, and 12 feet high. How many cubic feet of space does it have? _____

6. This is a diagram of the living room in a house. Compute the number of cubic feet in the room. (*Hint*: Do the problem in two sections.) _____

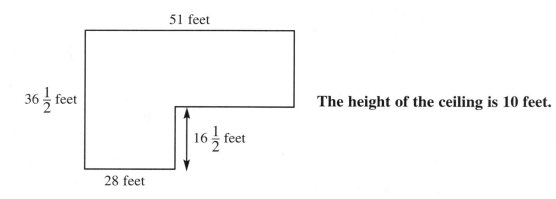

51 feet

$36\frac{1}{2}$ feet

The height of the ceiling is 10 feet.

$16\frac{1}{2}$ feet

28 feet

7. A city water tower is 83 feet high with a radius of 25 feet. How many cubic feet of water can be stored in the tower? _____

8. A cubic foot of water weighs 62.38 pounds. What is the weight of the water that can be stored in the water tower in problem #7? _____

9. One cubic foot of water equals 7.48 gallons. How many gallons of water can be stored in the water tower in problem #7? _____

10. How many cubic inches of water will fit into a hose which is 50 feet long and has a radius of $\frac{1}{2}$ inch? _____

11. One silo or elevator for storing grain has a radius of 15 feet and is 120 feet high. How many cubic feet of grain can be stored in it? _____

Facts to Know

- Two-step problems involve two operations.
- Multi-step problems involve more than two operations.

Five-Step Plan

1. Read the problem carefully. Make sure you understand what the situation is. Know who and what is involved.

2. State the problem to be solved. In your own words, briefly write or restate the problem.

3. Determine the operations to be used. Decide which of the four operations you need to do first and which numbers to use. Decide which of the four operations you need to do next and which numbers to use. If a third or fourth step is involved, determine which operation and the numbers to use.

4. Do the operations in order. Carefully recheck your calculations.

5. Check the final answer to see if it is reasonable.

Use the Five-Step Plan to solve these problems.

Sample

Jennifer bought a mountain bike priced at $299.00. She received a 20% discount because the dealer was overstocked. She had to pay an 8% sales tax on the amount she actually paid for the bike. What was the total cost of the bike, including tax?

Step 1: *Read the problem carefully.* Note that she gets a discount, but she has to pay sales tax.

Step 2: *State the problem.* The problem breaks down into four main sections:

A. How much money does the discount amount to? _____

C. How much tax must she pay? _____

B. How much does the bike cost after the discount? _____

D. What is the total cost of the bike, including tax? _____

Steps 3 and 4: *Determine the operations to be used. Do the operations.*

A. **Multiply** $299.00 by .20 (20%) to determine the amount of the discount.

$$\begin{array}{r} \$299.00 \\ \times \quad .20 \\ \hline \$59.8000 \ (\$59.80) \end{array}$$

C. **Multiply** the discounted cost of the bike $239.20 by .08 (8%) to determine the amount of tax.

$$\begin{array}{r} \$239.20 \\ \times \quad .08 \\ \hline \$19.1360 \ (\$19.14) \end{array}$$

B. **Subtract** the discount ($59.80) from $299.00 to determine the discounted cost of the bike.

$$\begin{array}{r} \$299.00 \\ - \quad \$59.80 \\ \hline \$239.20 \end{array}$$

D. **Add** the amount of the tax ($19.14) to the discounted cost of the bike to get the final answer, which is $258.34.

$$\begin{array}{r} \$239.20 \\ + \quad \$19.14 \\ \hline \$258.34 \end{array}$$

Step 5: Check the final answer to see if it is reasonable.

Frederica's Funky Fashions

Frederica's Funky Fashions is the newest clothing store in the mall with the trendiest clothes. They are having a spectacular sale with huge discounts on school styles and sports clothes for teenagers.

Directions: Use the information on page 25 to help you solve these problems.

1. Marlena bought 3 pairs of jeans, which usually sell for $19.00 each. They were on sale at 20% off the regular price. How much did Marlena spend? _____

2. James bought 7 T-shirts, which usually cost $6.50 each, on sale for 25% off the regular price. How much did he spend? _____

3. Elena bought 3 tops at $9.75 each and 4 pairs of shorts at $18.85 each. How much was her bill?

_____

4. Ricky bought 7 colored T-shirts at $4.95 each and 2 pairs of jeans at $13.75 each. He got a 30% discount on everything. How much money did he spend on clothes? _____

5. Roxanne spent $13.68. Joanne spent $27.98. Alyssa spent $33.87. Marie spent $22.34. Patricia spent $66.88. What was the average amount spent by the 5 girls? _____

6. Jimmy bought a jacket listed at $42.50 for $\frac{1}{2}$ off the price. He bought a pair of shorts listed at $12.00 for $\frac{1}{3}$ off the price. How much did he spend? _____

7. Melissa bought an outfit, which was supposed to cost $56.88 at a 40% discount. She had to pay 8% sales tax. How much did she spend for the outfit? _____

Directions: Use the information below to answer questions 8–11.

Frederica's Receipt Totals for One Week

Monday	Tuesday	Wednesday	Thursday	Friday	Saturday	Sunday
$22,567.89	$21,798.96	$28,455.02	$27,886.09	$38,997.66	$44,529.51	$29,654.32

8. What were the average daily earnings for this week at Frederica's? _____

9. Which two days of receipts approximately equaled one other day's sales? _____

10. These receipts included a sales tax of 8%. How much of the total weekly receipts were for taxes?

_____

11. How much more money did Frederica's make on the three days of the weekend (Friday, Saturday, Sunday) than on Monday through Thursday? _____

Boom Box City

Boom Box City offers the absolute latest in home entertainment appliances from big screen televisions to the largest boom box on the market.

Directions: Use the information on page 25 to help you solve these problems.

1. The Blast'em Boom Box with four speakers is listed at $144.95. You can get a 30% discount if you pay cash. How much will the boom box cost with the discount? _____

2. You can buy a standard VCR for $99.75 plus 8% tax. How much change would you receive from $120.00? _____

3. You could buy a DVD player for $179.67 or a DVD/CD player for $189.41. There is an 8% sales tax on each item. You have only $200 to spend. Which player can you afford to buy? _____ How much change would you have left? _____

4. A widescreen television is listed at $970.56. You can get a 25% discount if you buy it today. There is an 8% sales tax. How much will the television cost if you buy it today?
_____

5. You could buy a cordless phone answering machine for $129.88 or a traditional phone answering machine for $87.75 and a second phone for $30.89. Which system is cheaper and by how much?
_____

6. A small runner's headphone and cassette player costs $10.79. A CD player with headphones is listed at $49.99 but is offered at a 40% discount for today only. How much more than the cassette player would you pay for the CD unit if you bought it today? _____

7. You can purchase a home computer for $699.89. A separate monitor and printer will cost you $189.77 and $159.99, respectively. A complete system including all of these pieces is available for the purchase price of $999.89. How much would you save by purchasing the complete system? _____

8. A digital camcorder costs $299.99 plus an 8% sales tax at Boom Box City. The same machine can be purchased on the Internet for $349.45 with no sales tax. Which costs less money and by how much? _____

9. A complete sound system with a CD recorder costs $499.99. A home theater system costs $389.49. If you purchase both systems, you get a 40% discount and a $50.00 rebate from a manufacturer. How much less than the price of the sound system will it cost to buy both systems? _____

10. The original price of a television was $200. The sale price was $150. The discount was what percentage of the original price? _____

Vacation Time

Vacation time often involves lots of travel time and an opportunity to spend a great deal of money. Compute the answers to these vacation problems.

Directions: Use the information on page 25 to help you solve these problems. Use a calculator to check your computations, if your teacher approves.

1. You and your friends went on a bike hike through some very hilly terrain. You rode 22.5 miles on the first day, 34.7 miles on the second day, 16.25 miles on the third day, and 18 miles on the final day. What was your average number of miles per day?_____

2. During a camping trip, you were able to hike through the mountains at a speed of 100 feet every 5 minutes. How many hours and minutes would it take to hike 1 mile? (A mile is 5,280 feet.)____

3. You have to read a novel during vacation for your literature class. The book has an average of 10 words per line and 30 lines per page. There are 230 pages in the book. You read an average of 345 words per minute. How many hours and minutes will it take you to read the book? _____

4. You drove 380 miles from Los Angeles to San Francisco. Your trip started at 8:00 A.M. and ended at 5:30 P.M. How many miles did you average per hour?_____

5. The odometer on your family car read 35 when you started a trip from Seattle and 215 when you reached Portland 3 hours later. On average, how many miles did you travel each minute? (There are 60 minutes in 1 hour.)_____

6. It costs $44.75 to buy an entrance ticket to your favorite amusement park, the Screaming Meemies Roller Coaster Park. How much change would you receive from $200 to buy tickets for a family of 4? _____

7. An entrance ticket to Screaming Meemies Roller Coaster Park costs $44.75. If you arrived at the park at 10:00 A.M. and left at 12:00 midnight, what was the average hourly cost of your day at the park?_____

8. You spent $4.50 for a hamburger, $2.79 for fries, and $1.89 on a drink for lunch. How much change did you get from a $10.00 bill?_____

9. Your family dinner bill at a restaurant in the park came to $48.90. You added a 15% tip for the waitress. You had a $9.50 discount coupon. How much did you pay for dinner?_____

Facts to Know

Some problems can't be solved just by following a plan or looking for code words. The way these unconventional problems are written requires you to try different strategies until you hit on a reasonable solution. Sometimes you may have to try two or three different strategies before you hit on the correct approach.

In these problems follow these steps:

> 1. Read the problem carefully, twice.
> 2. State the problem to be solved in your own words.
> 3. Try each strategy until you get one that works.

Problem-Solving Strategies

Guess and Check

Your coach bought 7 balls. The baseballs cost $3.98 and the basketballs cost $19.98. The total cost was $75.86. How many baseballs and how many basketballs did he buy?

You know:

- the cost of each type of ball
- the total cost
- the number of balls purchased

You guess:

- 1 baseball ($3.98) plus 6 basketballs ($119.88) equals $123.86—too high
- 3 baseballs ($11.94) plus 4 basketballs ($79.92) equals $91.86—too high but closer
- 4 baseballs ($15.92) plus 3 basketballs ($59.94) equals $75.86—exactly right

Working Backwards

When Peter started selling greeting cards, he spent half of his money to buy the cards. Then he spent half of what he had left on advertising. He only has $50.00 now. How much money did he start with?

You know: **Check:**

- how much money he now has $200.00 divided by half is $100.00
- the fractional amount he spent each time $100.00 divided by half is $50.00

Work Backwards:

- He has $50.00 now.
- He had twice $50.00 ($100.00) before he spent half on advertising.
- He had twice $100.00 ($200.00) before he spent half on cards.

Make a Visual (chart, diagram, graph, list, or table)

There are four baseball teams in a league. How many games must be played so that each team plays every other team once and only once? There are six games altogether. Make a chart (or diagram):

- Team 1 plays Team 2   • Team 2 plays Team 3
- Team 1 plays Team 3   • Team 2 plays Team 4
- Team 1 plays Team 4   • Team 3 plays Team 4

Things to remember when using guess and check.

> 1. Read the problem carefully, twice.
>
> 2. State the problem to be solved in your own words.
>
> 3. Guess at an answer and check how close you are.
>
> 4. If possible, start with a number in the middle of a range of possible guesses.

Directions: Use the information on page 29 and the reminders above to help you solve these problems.

1. Danielle bought several tops for $9.50 each and some skorts (skirt/shorts) for $18.00 each. She spent $129.00 for 10 pieces. How many tops did she buy? How many skorts did she buy?

   Guess #1: tops _____ skorts _____

   Guess #2: tops _____ skorts _____

   Guess #3: tops _____ skorts _____

   Answer: tops _____ skorts _____

2. Liz has $0.93 in a total of nine coins. She does not have a half dollar. How many of each coin does she have?

   pennies _____ nickels _____ dimes _____ quarters _____

3. Albert found $1.41 in a total of nine coins in the sofa. What two combinations of coins could he have?

   A. pennies _____ nickels _____ dimes _____ quarters _____ half dollars _____

   B. pennies _____ nickels _____ dimes _____ quarters _____ half dollars _____

4. You did 60 math problems in five days. On each day you did 3 more problems than the day before. How many math problems did you do each day?

   Day 1 ____ Day 2 ____ Day 3 ____ Day 4 ____ Day 5 _____

5. On a five-day vacation trip by car, you traveled 50 miles farther each day than the day before. You traveled 2,000 miles. How many miles did you travel each day?

   Day 1 ____ Day 2 ____ Day 3 ____ Day 4 ____ Day 5 _____

6. A bag of sporting equipment has 14 balls. There are 2 times as many tennis balls as baseballs. There is 1 less basketball than there are baseballs. There are 3 footballs. How many balls of each type are in the bag?

   footballs_____ tennis balls_____ baseballs_____ basketballs_____

7. Jack's dad is 40 years old. Jack is 14 years old. How old will each of them be when his dad is twice as old as Jack?

   Jack _____ Dad _____

8. Marie is 13 years old and her mother is 35 years old. How old will each of them be when Marie is half of her mother's age?

   Marie _____ Mother _____

Things to remember when working backwards to solve problems.

> 1. Read the problem carefully, twice.
> 2. State the problem to be solved in your own words.
> 3. Work backwards from the end of the problem using the facts given.
> 4. Always check your answer by working forwards.

Directions: Use the information on page 29 and the reminders above to help you solve these problems.

1. Sandy went to the coolest clothing store in the mall, Frederica's Funky Fashions. She spent half of her money on a dance outfit she just had to have. She spent $100.00 of her remaining money on a pair of running shoes. Then she spent half of the money she had left on an outfit with the logo of her favorite singer. She had $40.00 remaining. How much money did she have to start?

   Work Backwards: ____$40.00 x 2_____

   Answer: _____

   Check: _____

2. Loretta uses beads to make wristbands for her friends. She lost $\frac{1}{2}$ of her beads when they fell on the grass on her way to school. She used 300 of the remaining beads to make a wristband for her sister and 250 beads to make a headband for a friend. She now has 800 beads left. With how many beads did she start?

   Work Backwards: _____

   Answer: _____

   Check: _____

3. Frederica's Funky Fashions had a pile of clothes on a sales table. There were twice as many shorts as jeans. There were 4 times as many blouses as there were jeans. There were half as many skirts as there were jeans. Half of the skirts were blue. There were 8 blue skirts. How many jeans, shorts, blouses, and skirts were in the pile and what was the total number of clothes on the table?

   Work Backwards: _____

   Answer: _____

   Check: _____

4. Melissa spent twice as much money as Doreen in Frederica's. Alyse spent half as much money as Doreen did. Christina spent half as much money as Alyse did. Elaine spent $12.00, which was half as much as what Christina spent. How much did each girl spend? How much did they spend altogether?

   Work Backwards: _____

   Answer: _____

   Check: _____

5. John is $1\frac{1}{2}$ years older than Brett. Robert is 5 years older than John. Raymond is $1\frac{1}{2}$ years younger than Brett. James is 2 years old. He is 1 year younger than Raymond. How old is each boy?

   Work Backwards: _____

   Answer: _____

   Check: _____

A visual can be a . . .

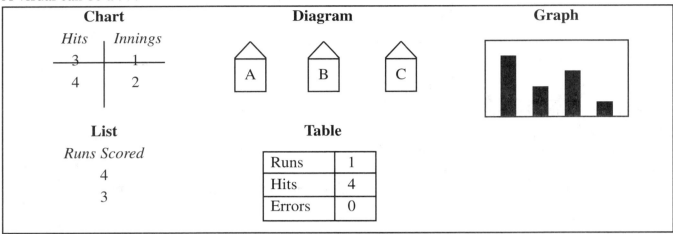

Directions: On another sheet of paper, use a visual to help you solve each of these problems.

1. A marathon runner ran one mile in 5 minutes, walked one mile in 8 minutes, and rested for one minute before repeating the pattern. At this rate, how long would it take the runner to cover 26 miles?

   Type of Visual: _____

   Answer: _____

2. There are 32 basketball teams in a middle school sudden death elimination tournament. The winning team in each contest goes on. How many games must be played to find the winning team?

   Type of Visual: _____

   Answer: _____

3. A baseball player got on base 9 times in every 17 at bats. How many times did he get on base in 153 at bats?

   Type of Visual: _____

   Answer: _____

4. The team mascot at Skunkfield Middle School was a striped skunk. The principal agreed to let the students name the mascot using any two of the following six names: Polecat, Stinker, Putrid, Fragrant, Sweety, and Scented. A name such as Polecat Sweety is different than Sweety Polecat. How many different name possibilities are there?

   Type of Visual: _____

   Answer: _____

5. A player on a middle school basketball team made 3 points in her first game. She made 2 more points than her first game in her second game and 3 more points than her second game in her third game. She continued to add 2 points and then 3 points in all of her succeeding games. In which game did she score 20 points? In which game did she score 35 points?

   Type of Visual: _____

   Answer: _____

6. In a middle school basketball tournament, six out of every 16 students are 12 years old, five are 13 years old, three are 11 years old, and two are 14 years old. There are 112 players in the tournament. How many players are 13 years old?

   Type of Visual: _____

   Answer: _____

Facts to Know

Many basic word problems can be expressed in an equation format, which makes it easy to understand and solve.

Using Algebraic Symbols

- You can use a letter of the alphabet to represent the unknown number in a problem.
- The equation is written so that the values on the left side of the equal sign equal the values on the right side of the equal sign.
- Solve the equation so that the unknown value represented by a letter is alone on one side of the equal sign and the value of the unknown is on the other side of the equal sign.

Sample A

Jennifer has $25.00. She needs $49.00 to buy a new school outfit. How much more money does she need?

Write an equation this way: n (money needed) + 25 (money she has) = 49 (cost of outfit)

Solve the equation by subtracting 25 from each side.

$$n + 25 = 49$$
$$n + 25 - 25 = 49 - 25$$
$$n = 24$$

Jennifer needs $24.00 more.

Axiom of Equality

- The axioms of equality were used to help solve the basic equation above.
- Any value added, subtracted, multiplied, or divided to one side of the equal sign must be added, subtracted, multiplied, or divided respectively to the other side.

Sample B

A group of 5 girls decided to split evenly the $18.75 cost of a CD album by their favorite group. How much money did each girl spend?

Write an equation.

Solve for n (the amount each girl spent) by dividing each side of the equation by 5.

$$5n = \$18.75$$
$$5n \div 5 = \$18.75 \div 5$$
$$n = \$3.75$$

Each girl spent $3.75.

Working with Two Unknown Quantities

You can use the same letter with an added or subtracted amount to represent two unknown quantities. Simplify and combine terms whenever possible.

Sample C

Sammy's mother is 2 years more than 3 times as old as Sammy. Their combined age is 42. How old are Sammy's mother and Sammy?

Equation: Let n equal Sammy's age. Let $3n + 2$ = Sammy's mother's age.

Since the total of their ages equals 42, then $n + 3n + 2 = 42$

Combine terms: $4n + 2 = 42$

Use the axioms of equality by subtracting 2 and then dividing by 4.

$$4n + 2 = 42$$
$$4n + 2 - 2 = 42 - 2$$
$$4n = 40$$
$$4n \div 4 = 40 \div 4$$
$$n = 10$$

Sammy is 10 years old. His mother is 32 years old.

Alex has $13.00 to buy a stereo that costs $24.00. How much more money does he need?
Write the equation. Let n = the amount of money.

$$n + 13 = 24$$

Use the axioms $n + 13 = 24$ Alex needs $11.00 more.
of equality: $n + 13 - 13 = 24 - 13$

$$n = 11$$

Directions: Use the information on page 33 to help you solve these problems. Write an equation for each word problem using n and solve it.

1. Jimmy is 23 years younger than his mom who is 36 years old. How old is Jimmy?

   Write the equation: _____

   Solve for n: _____

   Answer: _____

2. Albert has 15 CDs. Dianne has 2 more than 4 times as many CDs. How many CDs does Dianne have?

   Write the equation: _____

   Solve for n: _____

   Answer: _____

3. Joe's dad weighs 216 pounds. Joe weighs 122 pounds less than his dad. How much does Joe weigh?

   Write the equation: _____

   Solve for n: _____

   Answer: _____

4. Valerie took 25 shots in a basketball game. She had a 60% shooting percentage. How many shots did she make?

   Write the equation: _____

   Solve for n: _____

   Answer: _____

5. Sherrie's CD played for 22 minutes, which was 7 minutes longer than Matthew's CD. How long did Matthew's CD play?

   Write the equation: _____

   Solve for n: _____

   Answer: _____

6. Jerry read 1,145 words in five minutes. Jonathan read 316 words less in the same time period. How many words did Jonathan read?

   Write the equation: _____

   Solve for n: _____

   Answer: _____

7. Jeremiah rode 88 minutes on his skateboard without falling or getting off. Nick rode only $\frac{3}{4}$ as long. How long did Nick ride?

   Write the equation: _____

   Solve for n: _____

   Answer: _____

Extension

Write a word problem comparing your age to another person's age.

Word Problem: _____

_____

_____

Solve for n: _____

Answer: _____

Ronny's father is 24 years older than Ronny. Their combined age is 46. How old is Ronny? How old is Ronny's father?

Write the equation: Let x stand for Ronny's age. Let $x + 24$ stand for his dad's age.

Equation:

$$x + x + 24 = 46$$
$$2x + 24 = 46$$
$$2x + 24 - 24 = 46 - 24$$
$$2x = 22$$
$$2x \div 2 = 22 \div 2$$
$$x = 11$$

Ronny is 11.

His father is 35.

Directions: Use the information on page 33 to help you solve these word problems. Write an equation for each problem using n and then solve the problem.

1. Sarah's mother is 28 years older than Sarah is. Their combined age is 50. How old is Sarah? How old is her mother?

   Write the equation: _____

   Solve for n: _____

   Answer: _____

2. Joe's dad weighs 140 pounds more than Joe. Their combined weight is 336 pounds. How much does Joe weigh? How much does his dad weigh?

   Write the equation: _____

   Solve for n: _____

   Answer: _____

3. Christina has $22.00 more than 3 times as much money as Melissa has. Together they have $122.00. How much money does each girl have?

   Write the equation: _____

   Solve for n: _____

   Answer: _____

4. In a one-minute time period, Joseph read 2 times as many words as John. Together they read 669 words. How many words did each boy read?

   Write the equation: _____

   Solve for n: _____

   Answer: _____

5. Norman is 4 times as old as his brother Nicholas. Their combined age is 15. How old is each boy?

   Write the equation: _____

   Solve for n: _____

   Answer: _____

6. George has 9 times as many stamps in his collection as Daniel has. Bryan has 2 times as many stamps as Daniel. The combined stamp collection of the three boys is 144. How many stamps does each boy have?

   Write the equation: _____

   Solve for n: _____

   Answer: _____

Directions: Use the information on page 33 to help you solve these word problems. Write an equation for each problem using *n* and then solve the problem.

1. Fred's dad is 25 years older than Fred. His mother is 23 years older than Fred. The combined age of the three people is 93. How old is Fred? How old is each parent?

   Write the equation: _____ Solve for *n*: _____

   Answer: _____

2. A bike costs $100.00 more than a scooter. A scooter costs $60.00 more than a skateboard. The total cost of the 3 items is $310.00. How much is the skateboard? How much is the scooter? How much is the bike?

   Write the equation: _____ Solve for *n*: _____

   Answer: _____

3. Jimmy's brother is 9 times as old as Jimmy. In 6 years, his brother will be only 3 times as old as Jimmy. How old is each boy?

   Write the equation: _____ Solve for *n*: _____

   Answer: _____

4. Maybelle is 5 years younger than Jesse. Ellen is 2 years older than Jesse. Jeanne is 8 years older than Jesse. The combined age of the four children is 53.

   How old is Jesse? _____ How old is Maybelle?_____

   How old is Ellen? _____ How old is Jeanne?_____

   Write the equation: _____ Solve for *n*: _____

   Answer: _____

5. Elsa had $15.00 more than Joseph. Julian had $10.00 less than Joseph. Martha had $23.00 more than Joseph. Together they had $108.00. How much money did each student have?

   Write the equation: _____ Solve for *n*: _____

   Answer: _____

6. Christina had 2 times as much money as Melissa. Charmain had 4 times as much money as Melissa. Together they had $105.00. How much money did each girl have?

   Write the equation: _____ Solve for *n*: _____

   Answer:_____

7. Matthew had 3 times as much money as Kristin. Joshua had $10.00 less than Matthew did. Altogether they had $74.00. How much money did each person have?

   Write the equation: _____ Solve for *n*: _____

   Answer: _____

8. Kenneth is 8 years older than Andrew. Billy is 3 times as old as Andrew. Cameron is 5 years younger than Andrew. The combined age of the four is 63. How old is each boy?

   Write the equation: _____ Solve for *n*: _____

   Answer: _____

Facts to Know

Ratios

- A ratio is used to compare two numbers or the size of two amounts.
- A ratio can be used to compare part of something to the entire amount as you do in a fraction.
- A ratio can compare one part of a whole to another part of a whole.
- A ratio can compare all of one thing to all of something else.

Sample A

Kathy has 7 orange tennis balls and 5 yellow tennis balls.

The ratio of orange tennis balls to all tennis balls is $\frac{7}{12}$

The ratio of yellow tennis balls to all tennis balls is $\frac{5}{12}$

The ratio of orange tennis balls to yellow tennis balls is $\frac{7}{5}$

The ratio of yellow tennis balls to orange tennis balls is $\frac{5}{7}$

Writing Ratios

- A ratio can be written as a fraction: $\frac{2}{3}$
- A ratio can be expressed with a colon: 2:3.
- A ratio can be written with "to": 2 to 3.

Proportions

- A proportion is used to compare two ratios.
- A proportion is an equation which shows that two ratios are equal.
- A proportion can be written in fraction form. $\frac{1}{2} = \frac{5}{10}$
- A proportion can be written in colon form. 1:2 :: 5:10 (1 is to 2 as 5 is to 10)
- The outer terms (1 and 10) are called the *extremes*.
- The inner terms (2 and 5) are called the *means*.

Using Proportions

- The product of the means equals the product of the extremes.
- If you know any three of the terms, you can find the fourth.
- You can also solve a proportion by using cross products.

1:2 :: 5:10

$2 \times 5 = 10$ and $1 \times 10 = 10$

1:7 :: 4:c $1 \times c = c$

$7 \times 4 = 28$ $c = 28$

$\frac{4}{6} = \frac{8}{a}$ or $4 \times a = 6 \times 8$

$4a = 48$

$a = 12$

> **Some special formulas with rates are the following:**
>
> Rate of Speed = Distance divided by Time ($R = D/T$)
>
> Distance = Rate of Speed multiplied by Time ($D = R \times T$)
>
> Time = Distance divided by Rate of Speed ($T = D/R$)

Rates

A rate is a special ratio whose denominator is always 1.
Examples include miles per gallon (mpg) and miles per hour (mph).

Sample B

If you travel 40 miles in one hour, how far do you travel in 3 hours?

(miles) $\frac{40}{1} = \frac{d}{3}$ $d = 120$

(hours)   You travel 120 miles in 3 hours.

Directions: Use the information on page 37 to help you answer these questions. Use both forms of ratio in your answer. The first one is done for you.

1. Ratio of baseballs to golf balls <u>4/7</u> or <u>4:7</u>

   Ratio of baseballs to all balls <u>4/11</u> or <u>4:11</u>

   Ratio of golf balls to baseballs <u>7/4</u> or <u>7:4</u>

   Ratio of golf balls to all balls <u>7/11</u> or <u>7:11</u>

2. Ratio of jeans to shirts_____

   Ratio of jeans to clothes items _____

   Ratio of shirts to jeans_____

   Ratio of shirts to clothes items_____

3. Ratio of bicycles to skateboards_____

   Ratio of bicycles to wheeled vehicles_____

   Ratio of skateboards to bicycles_____

   Ratio of skateboards to wheeled vehicles _____

Directions: Write these rates as ratios as a fraction and with a colon. The first one is done for you. A rate always has a denominator of 1.

4. 60 miles per gallon

   <u>60/1</u> or <u>60:1</u>

5. 55 miles per hour

   _____ or _____

6. 16 ounces to a pound

   _____ or _____

7. 1,200 rpm (revolutions per minute)

   _____ or _____

8. 24 hours in a day

   _____ or _____

9. 60 minutes to an hour

   _____ or _____

10. 365 days to a year

    _____ or _____

11. 8% apr (annual percentage rate)

    _____ or _____

Directions: Use the information on page 37 to help you solve these word problems. Use an equation in either fraction or colon format to solve each problem. The first one has been done for you.

1. You can run a distance of 2 blocks in 3 minutes. How many blocks can you run in 18 minutes?

    Equation: $2{:}3 :: n{:}18$ or $2/3 = n/18$

    $$3 \times n = 2 \times 8$$
    $$3n = 36$$
    $$n = 12$$

    Answer: You can run 12 blocks.

2. You can read 5 pages of a novel in 3 minutes. How many pages of the novel can you read in 60 minutes?

    Equation: _____

    Answer: _____

3. It takes you 5 minutes to mow 7 square yards of a lawn. How long would it take to mow 630 square yards?

    Equation: _____

    Answer: _____

4. A running faucet sends 14 gallons of water down the drain every 3 minutes. How many gallons will go down the drain in 90 minutes?

    Equation: _____

    Answer: _____

5. A clothes washer uses 170 gallons of water for 4 loads. How many gallons would be used for 240 loads?

    Equation: _____

    Answer: _____

6. A volunteer beach clean up crew collected 20 bags of trash in 3 hours. How many hours would it take them to collect 1,000 bags of trash?

    Equation: _____

    Answer: _____

7. The average American uses about 145 pounds of paper every 3 months. How many pounds of paper are used in 24 months?

    Equation: _____

    Answer: _____

Solving Word Problems with Rates and Proportions

Directions: Use the information on page 37 to help you solve these word problems. Use an equation in either fraction or colon format to solve each problem.

1. If you travel at a speed of 55 miles per hour, how far will you travel in 7 hours?

   Equation: _____

   Answer: _____

5. Each month Americans throw away 2 million tons of leaves and grass. How many tons are thrown away in 48 months?

   Equation: _____

   Answer: _____

2. A car will travel 18 miles on 1 gallon of gasoline. How far will it travel on 20 gallons of gasoline?

   Equation: _____

   Answer: _____

6. A car traveled 2,980 miles between Boston and Los Angeles. The car traveled at an average speed of 40 miles per hour. How long did it take the car to travel this distance?

   Equation: _____

   Answer: _____

3. There are 60 minutes in 1 hour. How many minutes are there in $5\frac{1}{2}$ hours?

   Equation: _____

   Answer: _____

4. There are 24 hours in 1 day. How many hours are in 13.5 days?

   Equation: _____

   Answer: _____

7. A bicyclist traveled 100 miles in 9 hours. How many miles did she travel in 40.5 hours?

   Equation: _____

   Answer: _____

8. There are 16 ounces in 1 pound. How many ounces are there in a 45-pound dog?

   Equation: _____

   Answer: _____

Challenge

- There are 60 seconds in 1 minute. How many seconds are there in 1 day? _____
- There are 24 hours in 1 day. How many hours are there in 1 year? _____

Solving Word Problems with Data and Graphs

Bar Graph

Calories Burned Per Hour

1,000
900
800
700
600
500
400
300
200

Running | Cross-Country Skiing | Swimming | Bicycling | Tennis | Walking | Handball

Type of Exercise

Directions: Use the bar graph to answer these questions.

1. How many calories would you burn playing handball for one hour?_____
2. Approximately how many calories would you burn bicycling? _____
3. How many more calories would you lose running rather than playing tennis?_____
4. How many calories would you burn on a $2\frac{1}{2}$ hour cross-country skiing trip? _____
5. Which two activities are almost the same in terms of the amount of calories they burn?

   _____
6. Approximately how many calories would you burn after one hour of running and one hour of swimming?_____
7. Which two activities would have to be done for one hour each to equal one hour of cross-country skiing? _____
8. Would you burn more calories on a 3-hour walk or a 1-hour run? _____
9. Which exercise would be best for you?_____

Histogram

State Population (1995)

Number of States

24
22
20
18
16
14
12
10
8
6

under 1 million | 1–5 million | 5–10 million | over–10 million

Population

Directions: Use the histogram to answer these questions.

10. How many states have a population under a million? _____
11. How many states have a population over 10 million? _____
12. How many states have a population of 5 to 10 million? _____
13. What range of population is most common for the states?_____
14. Name two reasons you think states have such different population figures. _____
15. Which two states do you think have the most population and the least population?_____
16. In which category does your state fall?_____

Solving Word Problems with Graphs and Statistics

Multiple-Line Graph

Daily Temperatures
(High and Low)

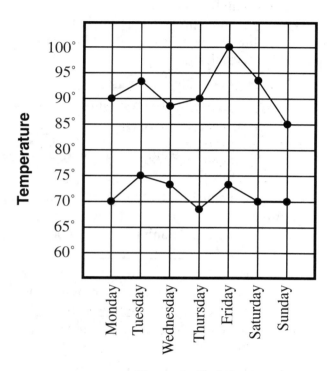

Day of the Week

Directions: Use the multiple-line graph to answer these questions.

1. Which day had the highest temperature of the week? _____

2. Which day had the lowest temperature that week? _____

3. What was the usual difference between high and low temperatures during this week? 15° to 20°? _____ 25° to 30°? _____ 3° to 4°? _____

4. On which day were the high and low temperatures exactly 20° apart? _____

5. On which two days were the lows 73°?
_____

6. On which two days were the highs 93°?
_____

7. On which three days were the lows 70°?
_____

8. What was the average high temperature for the week? _____

9. What was the average low temperature for the week? _____

10. How does this kind of graph help you analyze the temperature data? _____

Circle Graph

Percentage of Body Weight

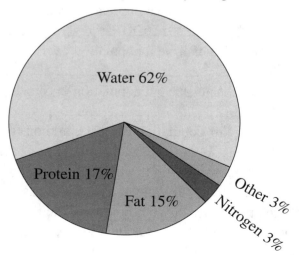

Directions: Use the circle graph to answer these questions.

11. Which component makes up the highest percentage of body weight?_____

12. Which single component on the graph has the lowest percentage of body weight?_____

13. What percentage of body weight do fat and protein make up together?_____

14. Where do you think calcium, sodium, and iron are included in the graph? _____

15. How much greater is the percentage of water than fat? _____

16. Where do you think the water is contained in the human body? _____

Brain Teasers

• • • • • • **Word Problems with Positive and Negative Numbers**

Less than Nothing

There are times when you not only have no money at all, you may owe money to a parent or friend. Negative numbers can be used to represent what you owe or how much you need just to get even. Negative numbers are also used in recording temperatures and golf games.

Directions: Apply your knowledge of integers (positive and negative numbers and zero) to help you solve these problems. Write an equation and then do the operations needed.

1. You bought a watch for $12.00. Since you only had $2.00, you had to borrow money from your mom. What negative number shows what you owe?

   Equation: <u>+ 2 – 12 = -10</u>
   Answer: <u>You owe $10.00</u>

2. The temperature when water freezes is 32° F. What temperature is 40° below freezing?

   Equation: _____
   Answer: _____

3. A golfer shot -4 (below par) on his first round of 18 holes. He shot an -11 on his second round and a -6 on his third round. How many shots below par was he after his three rounds?

   Equation: _____
   Answer: _____

4. The Acey Duecy Card Company owed the bank $1,000.00. They made a $750.00 payment to the bank. How much did they still owe the bank?

   Equation: _____
   Answer: _____

5. A player on a TV game show called Double Trouble! had -600 points because of some hard questions. He then answered several questions correctly. He received 200 points, 100 points, and 150 points. How many points did the player have? How many points did he need to get to 0?

   Equation: _____
   Answer: _____

6. One of the coldest temperatures ever recorded was -69° F in Utah in 1985. What temperature is 35° higher than -69° F?

   Equation: _____
   Answer: _____

7. The coldest temperature ever recorded was -129° F in Antarctica. The highest recorded temperature was 136° F in Africa. What is the difference?

   Equation: _____
   Answer: _____

8. A temperature of -80° F was recorded in Alaska. What is the difference between this reading and a high of 134° F recorded in Death Valley, California?

   Equation: _____
   Answer: _____

Directions: Using a word-processing software such as *Microsoft Word*® or *AppleWorks*®, create your own word puzzle maze along with a corresponding imaginative tale. Give your word puzzle maze to a friend or classmate and see if he or she can get the correct answers to solve the maze. A sample story is provided below. The corresponding maze is provided on the next page. Remember that the only way that the maze can be solved is by getting the correct answers to the questions asked in the story.

Rex lost his favorite bone. Help Rex find his missing bone by reading and solving the problems in the story below.

Rex misplaced his bone. He wants to go back to the last place he remembers seeing it: his dog house. But right now, Rex is hanging out with his buddies at the dog park. Before he leaves, Rex has to eat his fair share of the kibble. If he and four other dog friends are going to share 7.5 pounds of kibble, how much does each dog get?

After figuring this out, Rex has to make his way onto the bus to catch a ride back to his dog house. Rex has $1.35 with him. If the bus costs $0.75, how much change will he get back? While on the bus, he meets his neighbor, Gigi. Rex asks Gigi if she remembers seeing his bone. She responds that the last time she saw the bone was at her birthday party this year. Using today's standard calendar, Gigi is five years old, but in actual dog years, how old is she? (Hint: Remember, 1 human year = 7 dog years.)

Rex gets off the bus and finds that he wants to buy some water. A bowl of water costs $0.25. How much money will Rex have left after he buys the water? (Remember, he still has money left after he bought his bus fare.) Rex needs to walk the rest of the way to his dog house. If his house is 5 miles away and he can walk 1.5 miles per hour, how many hours will it take for Rex to get home?

After he finally makes it home, Rex looks inside his dog house. If his rectangular dog house is 5 ft x 7 ft, what is the area of Rex's house? When he takes a look inside his dog house, he still cannot find his bone.

Rex starts thinking about the last place he might have placed his bone. He finally remembers that he buried it in the backyard and promptly goes outside to dig it up. If it took Rex 35 minutes to dig up the bone and he began digging for it at 7:17 P.M., at what time did he finally find the bone? Rex was so happy that he finally found his bone.

Start

1.5 lbs.	2.0 lbs.	15 lbs.	86.2 lbs.	42 lbs.
65¢	60¢	30¢	71¢	0.4¢
25 yrs.	31 yrs.	35 yrs.	11.2 yrs.	7.1 yrs.
$1.20	10¢	35¢	9¢	99¢
2.33 mi.	1.13 mi.	2.45 mi.	3.33 mi.	3.12 mi.
20 ft.^{2}	15 ft.^{2}	23 ft.^{2}	35 ft.^{2}	77 ft.^{2}
3:41 A.M.	9:08 P.M.	7:44 P.M.	8:59 P.M.	7:52 P.M.

Finish

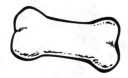

Answer Key

Page 6
1. change
   subtraction
   $2.12
2. money spent
   multiplication
   $36.64
3. split evenly
   division
   28 cards
4. amount needed
   subtraction
   $10.33
5. total cost
   addition
   $129.17
6. how much saved
   subtraction
   $2.21
7. total cost
   multiplication
   $41.58

Page 7
1. change
   subtraction
   $16.11
2. % discount
   multiplication
   $59.80
3. total cost
   addition
   $50.73
4. times as much
   multiplication
   $5,325
5. average
   division
   11.03 miles
6. total cost
   addition
   $1,342.97
7. times as much
   multiplication
   $350.10
8. total
   addition
   125.3 miles

Page 8
1. how much change
   subtraction
   $8.05

2. how much saved
   subtraction
   $6.95
3. product
   multiplication
   $113.85
4. how much left
   subtraction
   $25.41
5. split evenly
   division
   $1.59
6. share evenly
   division
   27 CDs
7. discount
   multiplication
   $3.19
8. difference
   subtraction
   $3.11

Page 10
1. addition
   $34.42
2. subtraction
   $2.55
3. subtraction
   $7.50
4. addition
   $40.47
5. subtraction
   $3.50
6. addition
   $78.41
7. addition
   Answers will vary.

Page 11
1. multiplication
   $45.00
2. division
   $3.75
3. multiplication
   $126.50
4. multiplication
   $99.80
5. multiplication
   $119.25
6. division
   $1.79
Challenge: $11.25; $8.75

Page 12
1. multiplication
   $22.68
2. addition
   $8.97
3. multiplication
   $59.67
4. addition
   $13.46
5. division
   $17.04
6. subtraction
   $2.70

Challenge:
   $70.20; 1 large
   cola, 1 Double Bean
   Burrito, 1 Tornado
   Taco; $0.39

Page 14
1. 1 1/2 miles
2. 5/12 miles
3. 2 2/3 miles
4. 1/3 mile
5. 1 1/6 miles
6. 8 miles
7. 1 1/4 miles
8. 4 5/18 miles
9. 1/2 mile
10. 26 2/3 miles

Extension: Answers will vary.

Page 15
1. 3/4 pizza
2. 10 cups
3. 3 3/4 pizzas
4. 1 1/2 pizzas
5. 1/2 pizza
6. 1/10 cake
7. 15/16 cake
8. 14 cups
9. 5/8 pizza
10. 81 ounces
11. 338 ounces
12. 1 1/2 ounces

Extension: 4 2/3 pizzas

Page 16
1. 33 3/4 miles
2. 39/40 mile

3. 7/10 mile
4. 1/2 lb.
5. 14 2/3 miles
6. 9 lbs.
7. 4 5/3 miles
8. 1 13/40 sec.
9. 12 3/8 miles
10. 7 17/24 miles

Extension: Answers will vary.

Page 18
1. $62.29; $237.71
2. $77.50; $160.21
3. $11.88; $148.33
4. $7.46; $29.82;
   $118.51
5. $57.94; $60.57
6. $10.00; $60.00;
   $0.57
7. $299.43
8. no

Page 19
1. 60%
2. 24 shots
3. 71% or 71.4%
4. 17 shots
5. 89% or 89.3%
6. 19 shots
7. 94% or 94.4%
8. 65% or 64.7%
9. 64% or 63.9%
10. 4 shots

Challenge: Answers will vary.

Page 20
1. 0.625 gallons
2. 25.2 lbs.
3. 4.4 oz.
4. 43.2 lbs.
5. 2.4 qts.
6. 114.7 lbs.
7. 19.5 lbs.
8. 3.75 or 3 3/4 times
9. 56% or 55.6%
10. 41%

Page 22
1. A. 314.5 sq. ft.
   B. 34.9 or
      35 sq. yd.

C. $698.00 or
$700.00
2. A. 185 sq. ft.
B. 5 rolls
C. $125
3. A. 244 3/8 sq. ft.
230 sq. ft.;
244 3/8 sq. ft.;
230 sq. ft.;
425 sq. ft.
B. 1,373 3/4 sq. ft.
or 1,374 sq. ft.
C. 4 gallons
D. $71.96

Page 23
1. A. 2,356 sq. ft.
B. $23.56
2. A. 200 ft.
B. $6.00
3. A. 1,116 sq. ft.
B. $11.16
4. A. 34.54 ft.
B. $1.04
C. 94.99 sq. ft.
D. $0.95
5. A. 643.75 sq. ft.
B. $96.56
6. A. 221 sq. ft.
B. $39.78
7. A. 37.68 ft.
B. 113.04 sq. ft.

Extension: Answers will
vary.

Page 24
1. 240 cartons
2. 4,070 cu. ft.
3. 25,688.34 cu. in.
4. 1,417.95 cu. cm
5. 370 cu. ft.
6. 14,820 cu. ft.
7. 162,887.5 cu. ft.
8. 10,160,922 lb.
9. 1,218,398.5 gallons
10. 471 cu. in.
11. 84,780 cu.ft.

Page 26
1. $45.60
2. $34.13
3. $104.65

4. $43.51
5. $32.95
6. $29.25
7. $36.86
8. $30,555.64
9. Monday and
Tuesday = Saturday
10. $17,111.16
11. $12,473.53

Page 27
1. $101.47
2. $12.27
3. You could buy the
DVD player;
$179.67
$5.96 change
4. $786.15
5. The traditional
machine/phone is
$11.24 cheaper.
6. $19.20
7. $49.76
8. Boom Box City
$25.46 less
9. $16.30
10. 25%

Page 28
1. 22.86 miles per day
2. 4 hr. 24 min.
3. 3 hr. 20 min.
4. 40 m.p.h.
5. 1 mile per minute
6. $21.00
7. $3.20
8. $0.82
9. $46.74

Page 30
1. 6 tops/4 skorts
2. 3 pennies, 3
nickels, 0 dimes, 3
quarters,
3. A. 1 penny, 0
nickels,
4 dimes,
4 quarters,
0 half dollars
B. 1 penny, 4
nickels,
2 dimes,

0 quarters,
2 half dollars
4. 6, 9, 12, 15, 18
5. 300, 350, 400, 450,
500
6. 3 footballs, 6 tennis
balls, 3 baseballs, 2
basketballs
7. Jack is 26 years
old; Dad is 52 years
old
8. Marie is 22 years
old; Mother is 44
years old

Page 31
1. $360.00
2. 2,700 beads
3. 240 total
16 skirts
32 jeans
64 shorts
128 blouses
4. $372.00 total
Elaine $12.00
Christina $24.00
Alyse $48.00
Doreen $96.00
Melissa $192.00
5. James 2 years old
Raymond 3 years
old
Brett 4 1/2 years
old
John 6 years old
Robert 11 years old

Page 32
1. 3 hr. 2 min.
2. 31 games
3. 81 times
4. 30 names
5. 20 points on 8th
game; 35 points on
14th game
6. 35 players are 13
years old

Page 34
1. $n = 36-23$
$n = 13$
13 years old
2. $n = (4 \times 15) + 2$

$n = 62$
62 CDs
3. $n = 216-122$
$n = 94$
94 lb.
4. $n = 25 \times .60$
$n = 15$
15 shots
5. $n = 22 - 7$
$n = 15$
15 minutes
6. $n = 1,145 - 316$
$n = 829$
829 words
7. $n = 88 \times 3/4$
$n = 66$
66 minutes

Extension: Answers will
vary.

Page 35
1. $n + (n + 28) = 50$
$2n + 28 = 50$
$n = 11$
Mother is 39 years
old.
Sarah is 11 years
old.
2. $n + (n + 140) = 336$
$2n + 140 = 336$
$n = 98$
Joe weighs 98 lbs.
Dad weighs 238
lbs.
3. $n + 4n + 22 = 122$
$n = 25$
Melissa has $25.00.
Christina has $97.00.
4. $n + 2n = 669$
$3n = 669$
$n = 223$
John read 223
words.
Joseph read 446
words.
5. $n + 4n = 15$
$5n = 15$
$n = 3$
Nicholas is 3 years
old.
Norman is 12 years
old.

6. $n + 9n + 2n = 144$
   $12n = 144$
   $n = 12$
   Daniel has 12 stamps.
   Bryan has 24 stamps.
   George has 108 stamps.

Page 36

1. $n + (n + 25) + (n + 23) = 93$
   $3n + 48 = 93$
   $n = 15$
   Fred is 15 years old.
   Mom is 38 years old.
   Dad is 40 years old.
2. $3n + 220 = 310$
   $n = 30$
   The skateboard is $30.
   The scooter is $90.
   The bike is $190.
3. $9n + 6 = 3(n + 6)$
   $n = 2$
   Jimmy is 2 years old.
   Brother is 18 years old.
4. $n + (n - 5) + (n + 2) + (n + 8) = 53$
   $4n + 5 = 53$
   $n = 12$
   Jesse is 12 years old.
   Maybelle is 7 years old.
   Ellen is 14 years old.
   Jeanne is 20 years old.
5. $n + (n + 15) + (n - 10) + (n + 23) = 108$
   $4n + 28 = 108$
   $n = 20$
   Joseph had $20.00.
   Elsa had $35.00.

Julian had $10.00.
Martha had $43.00.

6. $n + 2n + 4n = 105$
   $7n = 105$
   $n = 15$
   Melissa had $15.00.
   Christina had $30.00.
   Charmain had $60.00.
7. $n + 3n + (3n - 10) = 74$
   $7n - 10 = 74$
   $n = 12$
   Kristin had $12.00.
   Matthew had $36.00.
   Joshua had $26.00.
8. $n + (n + 8) + 3n + (n - 5) = 63$
   $6n + 3 = 63$
   $n = 10$
   Andrew is 10 years old.
   Kenneth is 18 years old.
   Billy is 30 years old.
   Cameron is 5 years old.

Page 38

1. 4/7 or 4:7
   4/11 or 4:11
   7/4 or 7:4
   7/11 or 7:11
2. 5/8 or 5:8
   5/13 or 5:13
   8/5 or 8:5
   8/13 or 8:13
3. 6/7 or 6:7
   6/13 or 6:13
   7/6 or 7:6
   7/13 or 7:13
4. 60/1 or 60:1
5. 55/1 or 55:1
6. 16/1 or 16:1
7. 1,200/1 or 1,200:1
8. 24/1 or 24:1
9. 60/1 or 60:1
10. 365/1 or 365:1
11. 8/100 or 8:100

Page 39

1. $2:3 :: n:18$
   $n = 12$ blocks
2. $5:3 :: n:60$
   $n = 100$ pages
3. $5:7 :: n:630$
   $n = 450$ minutes
4. $14:3 :: n:90$
   $n = 420$ gallons
5. $170:4 :: n:240$
   $n = 10,200$ gallons
6. $20:3 :: 1000:n$
   $n = 150$ hours
7. $145:3 :: n:24$
   $n = 1,160$ lb.

Page 40

1. $55:1 :: n:7$
   $n = 385$ miles
2. $18:1 :: n:20$
   $n = 360$ miles
3. $60:1 :: n:5.5$
   $n = 330$ minutes
4. $24:1 :: n:13.5$
   $n = 324$ hours
5. $2,000,000:1 :: n:48$
   $n = 96,000,000$ tons
6. $2,980:n :: 40:1$
   $n = 74.5$ hr.
7. $100:9 :: n:40.5$
   $n = 450$ miles
8. $16:1 :: n:45$
   $n = 720$ oz.

Challenge: 86,400 sec.; 8,760 hr.

Page 41

1. 600 calories
2. 650 calories
3. 400 calories
4. 2,500 calories
5. handball and bicycling
6. 1,650 calories
7. bicycling and walking
8. 3-hr. walk
9. Answers will vary.
10. 8 states
11. 7 states
12. 12 states
13. 1 to 5 million

14. Answers will vary.
15. California has the most.
    Wyoming has the least.
16. Answers will vary.

Page 42

1. Friday
2. Thursday
3. 15° to 20°
4. Monday
5. Wednesday and Friday
6. Tuesday and Saturday
7. Monday, Saturday, and Sunday
8. 91.7° or 92°
9. 71.7° or 72°
10. Answers will vary.
11. water
12. nitrogen
13. 32%
14. other category
15. 47%
16. Answers will vary.

Page 43

1. $+2 - 12 = -10$
   You owe $10.00.
2. $32 - 40 = -8$
   8 below 0
3. $-4 + -11 + -6 = -21$
   21 below par
4. $-\$1000 + \$750 = \$250$
   $250 owed
5. $-600 + 200 + 100 + 150 = -150$
   He needed 150 points to get to 0.
6. $-69 + 35 = -34°$ F
7. $-129 - (+)136 = -265$
   265° difference
8. $-80 - (+)134 = -214$
   214° difference